Hearts
COLORING BOOK

LINDSEY BOYLAN

Romantic Designs on a Dramatic Black Background

DOVER PUBLICATIONS, INC.
MINEOLA, NEW YORK

M000086209

Hearts big and small will fill you with inspiration as you explore the pages of this latest addition to the *Creative Haven* series. Birds and butterflies nestle around the whimsical heart designs, while fanciful botanicals weave through each frame. Dramatic black backgrounds will only help your ode to love, no matter what medium you choose. Specially designed for the experienced colorist, the illustrations in this book will provide you with endless opportunities to experiment with color combinations and technique. Each of the thirty-one plates has been perforated for removal to make displaying your work easy.

Copyright
Copyright © 2017 by Lindsey Boylan
All rights reserved.

Bibliographical Note
Hearts Coloring Book: Romantic Designs on a Dramatic Black Background is a new work, first published by Dover Publications, Inc., in 2017.

International Standard Book Number
ISBN-13: 978-0-486-80932-8
ISBN-10: 0-486-80932-3

Manufactured in the United States
80932301   2017
www.doverpublications.com

At the touch of love
everyone becomes a poet
Plato